I0644458

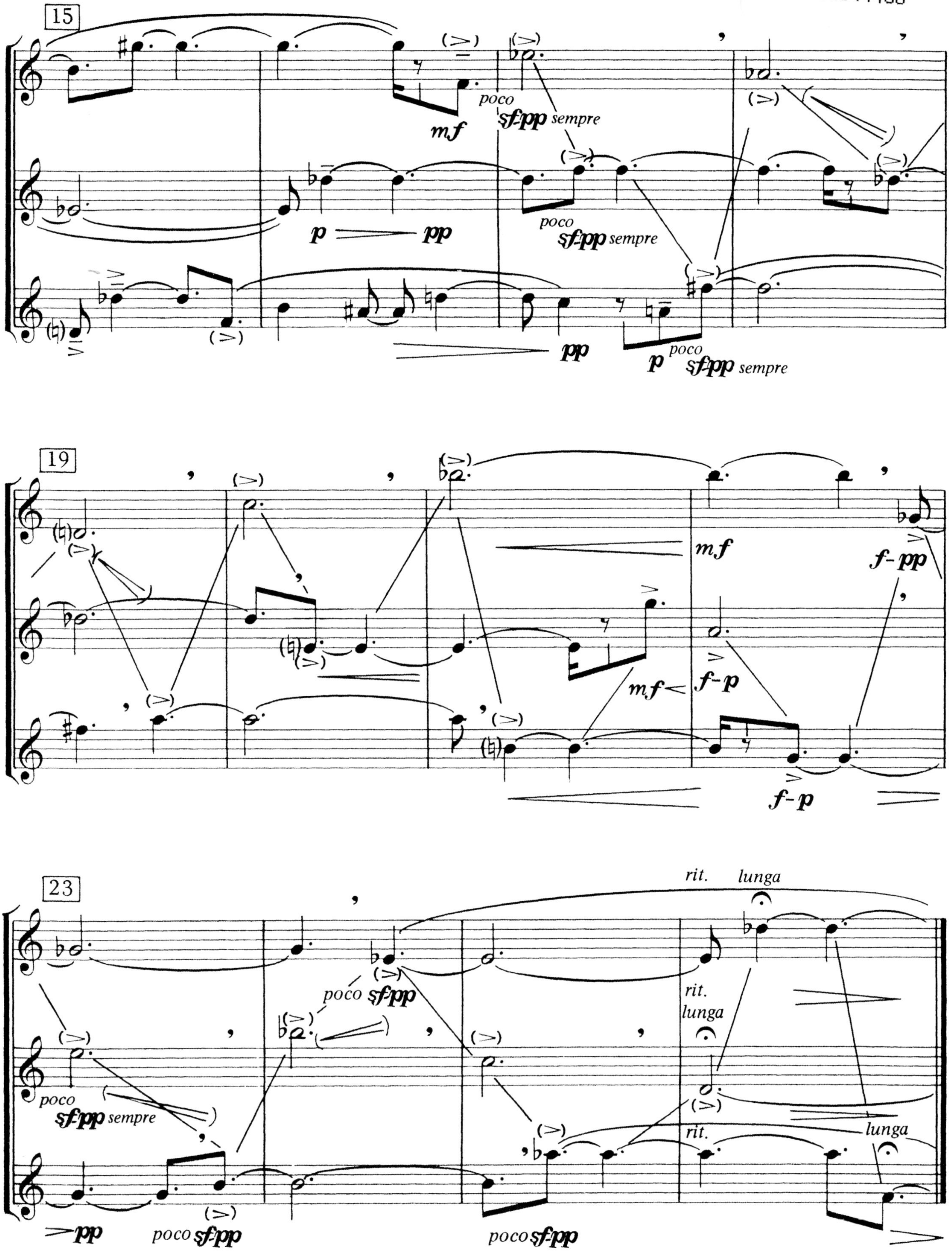
15
mf
poco
sf-pp sempre
p
pp
19
mf
f-pp
f-p
23
poco
sf-pp sempre
poco sf-pp
rit.
lunga

Canon for 3

In Memoriam Igor Stravinsky

Elliott Carter
(1971)

Playing Score
in B♭

AMP-7203

Printed in U.S.A.

ELLIOTT CARTER

CANON for 3

in Memoriam Igor Stravinsky

(for three equal instrumental voices)

G. SCHIRMER, *Inc.*

Note

The **Canon for 3 — In Memoriam Igor Stravinsky** (for three equal instrumental voices: at the augmented fourth by inversion and at the unison) was composed for one of the Stravinsky memorial issues of the English music magazine **Tempo**, at the request of David Drew, its editor.

In proposing the canonic form to a group of European and American composers, he was following the lead of Stravinsky himself, who wrote a number of commemorative pieces in this form.

This canon may be performed by three trumpets with different mutes; or by 1) muted trumpet, 2) clarinet, 3) oboe; or by any three instruments having the range of the score written in C.

To facilitate performance, this edition contains "playing scores" both in C and B♭.

Elliott Carter

1992 Printing

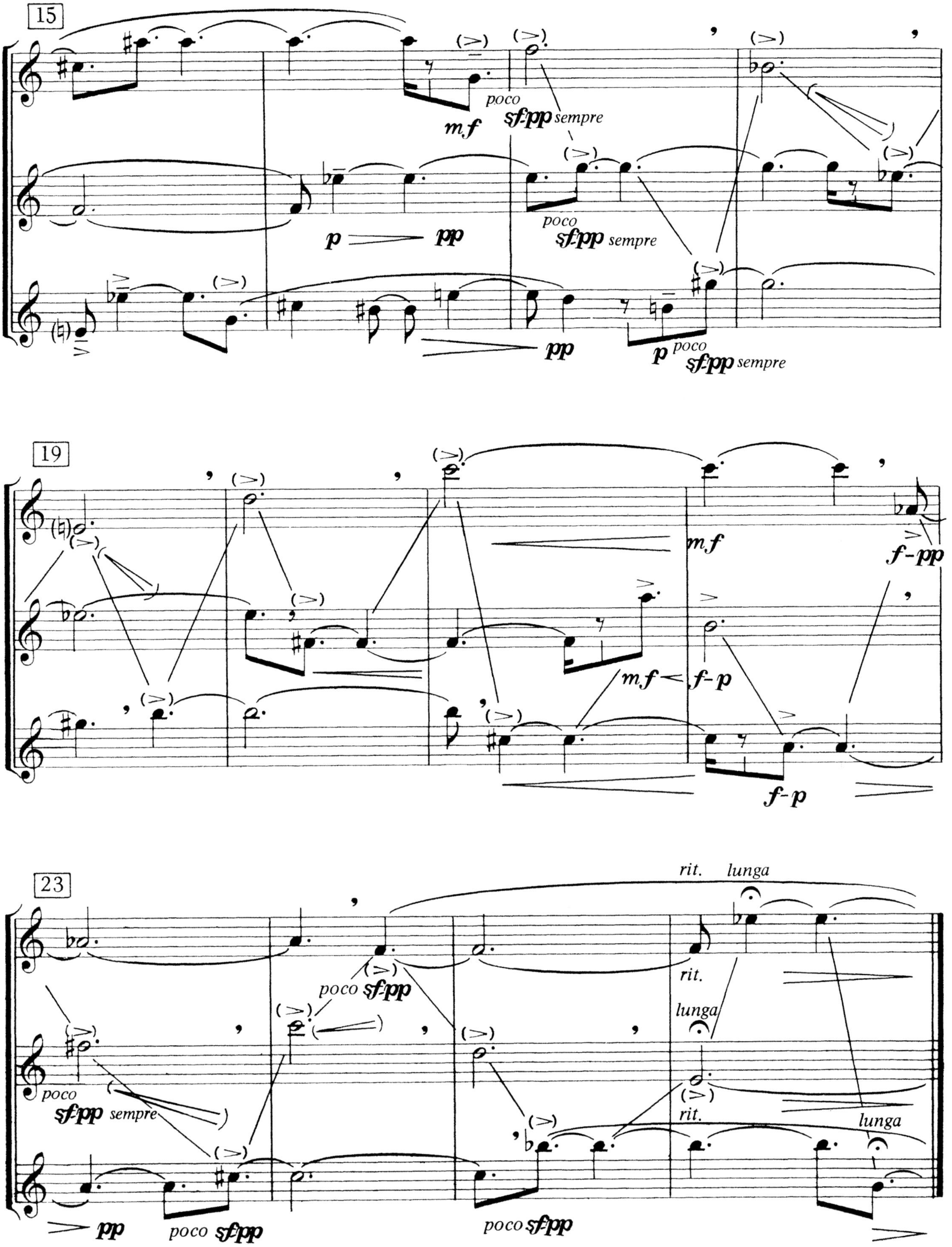
15
poco
sf-pp sempre
mf
p
pp
poco
sf-pp sempre
pp
p
poco
sf-pp sempre
19
mf
f-pp
mf
f-p
f-p
23
rit.
lunga
poco sf-pp
rit.
lunga
poco
sf-pp sempre
rit.
lunga
pp
poco sf-pp
poco sf-pp

Canon for 3

In Memoriam Igor Stravinsky

Playing Score
in C

Elliott Carter
(1971)

AMP-7203

Chamber Music of Elliott Carter

Brass Quintet (1974) 17' .... Parts 50226320 Score 50238490
Canon for Three (1971) (In Memoriam Igor Stravinsky) for equal instrumental voices 2' .... Score 50235490
Canonic Suite (1939, rev. 1945) for four clarinets 7' .... Parts 50234860 Score 50237310
Canonic Suite (1939, rev. 1981) for four alto saxophones 7' .... Score and Parts 50228360
Duo (1973-74) for violin and piano 18' .... Score and Part 50226350
A Fantasy About Purcell's "Fantasia upon One Note" (1974) .... Parts 50226490 Score 50238540
for brass quintet 3'
A Mirror on Which to Dwell (1975) for soprano and chamber orchestra* 20' .... Score 50238610

1. Anaphora
2. Argument
3. Insomnia
4. O Breath
5. Sand Piper
6. View of the Capitol from the Library of Congress

(Text: Elizabeth Bishop)

Night Fantasies (1980) for piano solo 24' .... Score 50236290
Tarantella (1936) for men's chorus and piano (4 hands) (Text: Ovid [Latin]) 8' .... Score 50226760
Three Poems of Robert Frost (1943) for medium voice and piano 6' .... Score 50249350

1. Dust of Snow
2. The Rose Family
3. The Line-Gang

(Text: Robert Frost)

Sonata (1952) for flute, oboe, cello, and harpsichord 18' .... Score and Parts 50224940
Sonata (1948) for cello and piano 22' .... Score and Part 50227330
String Quartet No. 1 (1950-51) 45' .... Parts 50227260 Score 50237060
String Quartet No. 2 (1959) 22' .... Parts 50488558 Score 50480491
String Quartet No. 3* (1971) 22' .... Score 50238300
Syringa* (1978) for mezzo-soprano, bass, and guitar with ensemble 20' .... Score 50238740
(Text: John Ashbery-English, ancient Greek)
Tell Me Where Is Fancy Bred (1938) for medium voice and guitar (Text: Shakespeare) 3' .... Score 50225820
Voyage (1943) for medium voice and piano (Text: Hart Crane) 8' .... Score 50225880
Woodwind Quintet (1948) 8' .... Parts 50223720 Score 50237000
8 Etudes and a Fantasy (1949-50) for woodwind quartet 23' .... Parts 50235020 Score 50237430
8 Pieces for Four Timpani (1950-66) 1 player 22' .... Score 50234240

* Performance material is available on rental.

U.S. $6.99
0 73999 95789 1
HL50235490

G. SCHIRMER, *Inc.*
DISTRIBUTED BY
HAL•LEONARD® CORPORATION
7777 W. BLUEMOUND RD. P.O. BOX 13819 MILWAUKEE, WI 53213

ISBN 978-0-7935-1432-8
9 780793 514328